TABLE OF CONTENTS

CHICKEN

TURKEY

PORK

BEEF

TABLE OF CONTENTS

DISCLAIMER

The information contained in this book is for general information purposes only. The authors and publishers of the Book make no representations or warranties of any kind, express or implied, about the completeness, accuracy, reliability, suitability, or availability with respect to the Book or the information, products, services, or related graphics contained in the Book for any purpose. Any reliance you place on such information is therefore strictly at your own risk.

In no event will the authors or publishers be liable for any loss or damage including without limitation, indirect or consequential loss or damage, or any loss or damage whatsoever arising from loss of data or profits arising out of, or in connection with, the use of this Book.
Through this Book you are able to link to other websites which are not under the control of the authors or publishers. We have no control over the nature, content, and availability of those sites. The inclusion of any links does not necessarily imply a recommendation or endorse the views expressed within them.

Every effort is made to keep the Book up and running smoothly. However, the authors and publishers take no responsibility for, and will not be liable for, the Book being temporarily unavailable due to technical issues beyond our control.
The recipes in this Book are provided as-is and may not have been tested in all situations or environments, which may impact the results based on various factors, such as altitude, climate, freshness of ingredients, etc. The authors and publishers are not responsible for any adverse reactions, effects, or consequences resulting from the use of any recipes or suggestions herein or procedures undertaken hereafter.

This Book does not provide medical or dietary advice. All nutritional information in the Book is provided as a courtesy and should not be construed as a guarantee. Readers should consult their physician or a qualified health professional on any matters regarding their health and well-being, or on any opinions expressed within the Book. The authors and publishers expressly disclaim responsibility for any adverse effect that may result from the use or application of the information contained in this Book.

By using this Book, you agree to indemnify and hold harmless the authors and publishers from any claim, loss, damage, or expense (including legal fees) attributed to your use of the recipes and information provided herein.

Please note that the cooking instructions and ingredient listings are meant as a guide and should be adjusted based on individual equipment and preference. Always exercise caution and common sense in the kitchen.

★I HOPE YOU LIKE IT ★

- **INTERESTED IN FOLLOWING A HEALTHY AND DELICIOUS DIET?**

- LOVE FULL COLOR PICTURES AND DESCRIPTIVE RECIPES?

★SCAN TO SEE MY OTHER DEICIOUS COOOKBOKS!★

DEMYSTIFYING THE AIR FRYER: SETTINGS AND SAFETY

- **Temperature:** Ranges from 180°F (82°C) to 400°F (204°C). Higher settings create crispier outcomes.
- **Timer:** Set for half of a typical oven's time. Due to fast air circulation, foods cook quickly. Keep an eye on early uses.
- **Preset Programs:** Many fryers have built-in settings for common items like fries or chicken.
- **Shake Reminder:** Some devices signal when to shake for even cooking. If not, set a midway reminder.
- **Ventilation:** Position your fryer away from walls. This ensures safety and optimal function.
- **Avoid Overfilling:** Too much food can result in uneven cooking. Portion appropriately.
- **Handle Safely:** Basket handles heat up. Use oven mitts, especially during cooking.
- **Oils:** Avoid aerosol sprays; they might degrade the non-stick layer. Opt for a mister with regular oil.
- **Cleaning:** Allow your fryer to cool down before cleaning. This prevents potential damage.
- **Regular Checks:** Always inspect before use, paying attention to cords and the heating element.

ESSENTIAL TOOLS AND ACCESSORIES

Baking Pans: Specifically designed for air fryers, these pans are perfect for baking cakes, muffins, or even quiches. They ensure even cooking and fit snugly inside the fryer.

Silicone Muffin Cups: Making individual servings of baked goods is a breeze with these cups. They are non-stick, heat-resistant, and easy to clean.

Grill Racks: Enhance your fryer's capacity with these racks, allowing for multiple layers of food, such as meats or vegetables, to be cooked simultaneously.

Non-stick Cooking Mats: These mats provide a smooth surface, ensuring smaller foods don't fall through the fryer's grid. They're ideal for items like cut vegetables or delicate fish.

Parchment Liners: An absolute savior for easier cleanup, these liners prevent food from sticking to the fryer's base.

Oil Sprayers: Get an even coat of oil on your foods using these misters. They provide controlled spritzing, WITH healthier cooking with less oil.

Skewers: Perfect for making kebabs or holding together stuffed meats, these can be made of metal or bamboo.

Silicone Tongs: Protect the non-stick layer of your fryer with silicone-tipped tongs. They're great for flipping and retrieving food without scratching the surface.

Air Fryer Cookbooks: For those new to air frying or looking to expand their repertoire, these books are filled with delicious, optimized recipes.

3 WHY AIR FRYER? BENEFITS UNVEILED

1. *Healthier Cooking:* The air fryer's claim to fame is its ability to produce crispy, fried-like textures with a fraction of the oil. By using hot circulating air, it cuts down fat content by up to 80%.

2. *Faster Meals:* In today's fast-paced world, the air fryer delivers quicker meals by heating up instantly and reducing cooking time, often cooking foods faster than conventional ovens.

3. *Versatility:* Beyond frying, the air fryer can roast, grill, bake, and even dehydrate. From crispy fries to moist cakes, its range is truly impressive.

4. *Energy Efficiency:* Air fryers use less energy compared to traditional ovens. They heat up rapidly and retain heat effectively, resulting in shorter cooking times and energy savings.

5. *Safety:* Built-in timers, auto shut-offs, and cool-touch exteriors minimize risks associated with forgetting a running oven or accidental burns.

6. *Space-saving:* For those with limited kitchen space, its compact design is a godsend. It fits comfortably on countertops, making it ideal for smaller kitchens or apartments.

7. *Less Odor:* Say goodbye to the lingering smell of fried oil. Air fryers are designed to contain odors, ensuring your kitchen remains fresh.

8. *Easy Clean-Up:* With non-stick surfaces and dishwasher-safe parts, the cleanup process is streamlined, leaving more time for enjoyment.

THE SCIENCE OF AIR FRYING

- **Rapid Air Circulation:** The core principle of air frying revolves around the circulation of hot air. High-speed fans circulate the hot air around the food, ensuring it cooks uniformly and achieves a crispy outer layer akin to traditional frying.

- **Reduced Fat Content:** Air fryers require a fraction of the oil used in deep frying. As a result, foods retain less oil, translating to fewer calories and fats, promoting healthier eating.

- **Enhanced Safety:** Without the need for large oil quantities, the risks associated with deep frying, such as oil splatters or potential burns, are significantly minimized.

- **Quick Cooking Times:** Due to the efficient heat distribution, air frying often reduces cooking time, making it a faster alternative to other cooking methods.

- **Crunch Factor:** The rapid air technology ensures the exterior of the food crisps up quickly, locking in moisture and achieving the sought-after crunch of fried foods without excess grease.

- **Environmentally Friendly:** With no oil disposal necessary, air frying is a more environmentally conscious choice.

- **Consistent Results:** Uniform heat distribution guarantees even cooking, ensuring consistent, restaurant-quality results.

5 COMMON MISTAKES AND HOW TO AVOID THEM

- **Overcrowding the Basket:** A cardinal mistake many make is jam-packing the air fryer basket. This hinders proper air circulation, leading to unevenly cooked food.

- **Neglecting Preheating:** Just like an oven, an air fryer benefits from preheating. Avoidance Tip: Spend an extra couple of minutes letting your air fryer reach the desired temperature. It'll be worth the wait!

- **Using Excessive Oil:** More oil doesn't necessarily mean crispier results. Avoidance Tip: A light mist or brush of oil is often enough. Remember, some foods, especially meats, release their fats.

- **Not Shaking Midway:** Some foods, like fries or veggies, might stick together. Avoidance Tip: A quick shake or stir halfway can ensure even browning and prevent clumping.

- **Setting Wrong Temperatures:** Too hot can lead to burnt exteriors with raw interiors. Avoidance Tip: Always consult a recipe or guide, and remember: it's easier to add more time than to remedy overcooked food.

- **Skipping Cleaning:** Neglected food residue can cause smoke or affect flavors. Avoidance Tip: After cooling, always clean the basket and interior. A quick wipe-down can go a long way.

- **Being Impatient:** Opening the fryer too often can cause the device to lose heat.

GLOSSARY OF CROCKPOT TERMS

- *Preheating:* The act of letting the air fryer run for a few minutes before cooking, allowing it to reach the desired temperature.

- *Air Circulation:* The process of hot air moving rapidly around the food in the air fryer, leading to faster and even cooking without much oil.

- *Misting:* Spraying a fine layer of oil onto the food or the basket, ensuring crispiness without drenching in fat.

- *Shake Reminder:* A feature in some air fryers that signals when it's time to shake the basket for even cooking.

- *Non-Stick Coating:* A surface finish in many air fryer baskets to prevent food from sticking.

- *Ventilation:* Essential in releasing hot air from the appliance. Ensures the device doesn't overheat and maintains efficient cooking.

- *Capacity:* Refers to the amount of food or volume an air fryer can handle, often measured in quarts or liters.

- *Preset Programs:* Built-in settings for popular dishes, taking the guesswork out of cooking times and temperatures.

- *Manual Turn*: The act of manually shaking or turning food for even cooking, especially if the fryer lacks a shake reminder.

CILANTRO-LIME CHICKEN WINGS

200 KCAL

2 SERVINGS

15 MIN

INGREDIENTS

- A handful of chicken wings (let's say, around 6-8 pieces)
- 1 lime (you'll need its zest and juice)
- A bunch of fresh cilantro (or coriander, whatever you call it!)
- A touch of olive oil (just a teaspoon)
- Salt to taste (not too much, okay?)
- A sprinkle of black pepper

DIRECTIONS

1. In a bowl, combine lime zest, juice, chopped cilantro, olive oil, salt, and black pepper. Mix it all up!
2. Toss the chicken wings in this zesty mixture. Let 'em soak in all that flavor for about 10 minutes.
3. Preheat your air fryer to 180°C (360°F). Once heated, place the marinated wings inside.
4. Cook for 12-15 minutes, until they're golden and crispy.
5. Serve hot! Maybe with a side salad?

NUTRITION

- **CARBS: 3g**
- **PROTEIN: 25g**
- **FAT: 10g**
- **FIBER: 1g**
- **OMEGA 3: 0.4g**
- **VITAMIN D: 0.5µg**
- **CALCIUM: 30mg**
- **IRON: 1.5mg**

ALLERGENS & TIPS

Allergens: Might contain traces of gluten (from cross-contamination).

Tips: Hey, if you're feeling a bit adventurous, why not toss in a pinch of chili flakes to that marinade? A little kick never hurt!

230 KCAL

2 SERVINGS

20 MIN

TERIYAKI CHICKEN THIGH BITES

INGREDIENTS

- 2 chicken thighs, bite-sized
- 3 tbsp low-sodium teriyaki sauce
- A smidgen of olive oil
- Sesame seeds for garnish
- Chopped spring onions for flair

DIRECTIONS

1. Combine chicken and teriyaki sauce in a bowl; let them get acquainted for 10 minutes.
2. Swirl in the olive oil, mixing well.
3. Preheat air fryer to 180°C (360°F). Place chicken pieces inside and cook for 10 minutes, remembering to flip halfway.
4. Once golden and delicious, top with sesame seeds and spring onions.

NUTRITION

- **CARBS: 8g**
- **PROTEIN: 28g**
- **FAT: 5g**
- **FIBER: 0.4g**
- **OMEGA 3: 0.1g**
- **VITAMIN D: 0.9µg**
- **CALCIUM: 20mg**
- **IRON: 1.1mg**

ALLERGENS & TIPS

Allergens: Contains soy (from teriyaki sauce) and sesame seeds.

Tips: Overnight marinating elevates flavor, and substituting teriyaki sauce is easy with soy sauce, a touch of honey, and a splash of vinegar; for some heat, add chili flakes.

SPICED TURMERIC CHICKEN TENDERS

190 KCAL

2 SERVINGS

15 MIN

INGREDIENTS

- 4 chicken tenders, lean & trimmed
- 1 tsp turmeric powder
- A pinch of black pepper
- 1/2 tsp paprika (gives a bit of a kick)
- 1/4 tsp garlic powder
- Light drizzle of olive oil
- Fresh coriander, for that touch of green

DIRECTIONS

1. In a cool mixing bowl, mix turmeric, pepper, paprika, and garlic powder.
2. Toss the chicken tenders in the mix, ensuring they're well-coated.
3. Lightly brush them with olive oil; helps in crisping.
4. Fire up your air fryer at 180°C (360°F) and slide the tenders in. Cook 'em for 12 minutes, making sure to turn at the halfway point.
5. Once golden and tempting, sprinkle fresh coriander on top.

NUTRITION

- **CARBS: 3g**
- **PROTEIN: 24g**
- **FAT: 8g**
- **FIBER: 1g**
- **OMEGA 3: 0.2g**
- **VITAMIN D: 1.5µg**
- **CALCIUM: 15mg**
- **IRON: 1.2mg**

ALLERGENS & TIPS

Allergens: None but always check your turmeric for additives.

Tips: A dollop of yogurt on the side adds a creamy contrast, and marinating for an hour can up the flavor game.

13

MEDITERRANEAN OLIVE-OIL DRIZZLED CHICKEN

180 KCAL

2 SERVINGS

20 MIN

INGREDIENTS

- 2 lean chicken breasts
- 2 tbsp extra virgin olive oil (the good stuff!)
- 1 tsp dried oregano
- 1/2 tsp garlic powder (or fresh garlic, your choice)
- Zest of 1 lemon
- Salt, to taste
- Fresh parsley, a handful

DIRECTIONS

1. In a bowl, mix olive oil, oregano, garlic, lemon zest, and a pinch of salt.
2. Give the chicken a nice dip into this sunny concoction.
3. Preheat the air fryer to 180°C (350°F).
4. Nestle chicken in, cooking for about 15 minutes. Turn once for that even golden hue.
5. Finish off with parsley – because, why not?

NUTRITION

- **CARBS: 1g**
- **PROTEIN: 26g**
- **FAT: 9g**
- **FIBER: 0.5g**
- **OMEGA 3: 0.1g**
- **VITAMIN D: 1.2µg**
- **CALCIUM: 12mg**
- **IRON: 0.9mg**

ALLERGENS & TIPS

Allergens: Contains olive oil, which can sometimes contain traces of tree nuts or other allergens depending on the brand.

Tips: Pair with a Mediterranean salad and a hint of feta – takes it to a new level!

MAPLE-SRIRACHA CHICKEN DRUMETTES

210 KCAL

2 SERVINGS

25 MIN

INGREDIENTS

- 6 chicken drumettes, skin removed
- 2 tbsp pure maple syrup
- 1 tbsp sriracha (add more if you dare!)
- 1/2 tbsp low-sodium soy sauce
- 1 garlic clove, minced
- A sprinkle of sesame seeds (for garnish)
- Fresh chives, finely chopped (also for garnish)

DIRECTIONS

1. Mix maple syrup, sriracha, soy sauce, and garlic in a bowl.
2. Toss drumettes in the mix, ensuring they're well-coated.
3. Fire up the air fryer to 180°C (350°F).
4. Place those lovely drumettes in and cook for 20 minutes. Flip 'em halfway for even crispiness.
5. Once done, sprinkle with sesame seeds and chives.

NUTRITION

- **CARBS: 10g**
- **PROTEIN: 22g**
- **FAT: 6g**
- **FIBER: 0.3g**
- **OMEGA 3: 0.2g**
- **VITAMIN D: 1.1µg**
- **CALCIUM: 18mg**
- **IRON: 0.8mg**

ALLERGENS & TIPS

Allergens: Contains soy.

Tips: Use organic maple syrup if you can – tastes even better and it's a healthier option!

15

GARLIC HERB CHICKEN MINI ROAST

320 KCAL
2 SERVINGS
3 MIN

INGREDIENTS

- 2 chicken breast halves
- 2 garlic cloves, minced
- 1 tbsp olive oil (choose a good one!)
- 1/2 tsp dried rosemary
- 1/2 tsp dried thyme
- Salt and pepper to taste

DIRECTIONS

1. Mix garlic, olive oil, rosemary, thyme, salt, and pepper in a small bowl.
2. Rub the herb mixture all over the chicken breasts.
3. Preheat air fryer to 175°C (345°F).
4. Pop the chicken in and air fry for 20 minutes, until golden brown and cooked through.
5. Let it rest a few minutes before slicing.

NUTRITION

- **CARBS: 3g**
- **PROTEIN: 28g**
- **FAT: 7g**
- **FIBER: 0.4g**
- **OMEGA 3: 0.1g**
- **VITAMIN D: 0.9µg**
- **CALCIUM: 15mg**
- **IRON: 0.7mg**

ALLERGENS & TIPS

Allergens: None in this simple recipe.

Tips: Try using fresh herbs if you've got them handy; they'll boost the flavor big time!

205 KCAL

2 SERVINGS

25 MIN

ROSEMARY ORANGE ZEST CHICKEN WINGS

INGREDIENTS

- Chicken wings (about 10 pieces, cause sharing is caring)
- Zest of 1 orange (let's get that citrus kick!)
- 2 sprigs fresh rosemary, finely chopped (the fresher, the better)
- 1 tbsp olive oil (trust me, it's all the fat you need)
- A pinch of salt and pepper (for that classic seasoning)

NUTRITION

- **CARBS: 4g**
- **PROTEIN: 22g**
- **FAT: 9g**
- **FIBER: 0.3g**
- **OMEGA 3: 0.2g**
- **VITAMIN D: 1µg**
- **CALCIUM: 20mg**
- **IRON: 1mg**

DIRECTIONS

1. In a mixing bowl, toss together orange zest, chopped rosemary, olive oil, salt, and pepper. It's gonna smell divine!
2. Add the chicken wings and give them a good mix. Make sure they get all cozy with the marinade.
3. Fire up your air fryer to 180°C (360°F). I know you're eager, but let it warm up.
4. Carefully place the wings in the fryer. Cook for about 20 minutes or till they're golden and crispy. Midway, give 'em a flip.
5. Take them out, let them cool for a bit, and dive in!

ALLERGENS & TIPS

Allergens: Be wary if you have citrus allergies because of the orange zest.

Tips: You can toss the wings in a bit of leftover orange juice after frying for a more intense citrus flavor. Trust me, it's a game-changer!

ALMOND-CRUSTED TURKEY PATTIES

180 KCAL

2 SERVINGS

20 MIN

INGREDIENTS

- 7 oz (200g) lean turkey mince
- 1.4 oz (40g) ground almonds
- 1 small onion, finely chopped
- 1 garlic clove, crushed
- A little fresh parsley, chopped
- A tad bit of sea salt and black pepper
- 1 tsp (5 ml) olive oil

DIRECTIONS

1. In a relaxed bowl mix, put together turkey, onion, garlic, parsley, salt, and pepper.
2. Mould into two chilled-out patties.
3. Coat them gently in almond grounds.
4. Preheat the air fryer to 360°F (180°C).
5. Gently brush with olive oil and lay them in.
6. 10 minutes on one side, flip, and another 8 minutes should do the trick.

NUTRITION

- **CARBS: 6g**
- **PROTEIN: 25g**
- **FAT: 6g**
- **FIBER: 2g**
- **OMEGA 3: 0.1g**
- **VITAMIN D: 0.5µg**
- **CALCIUM: 50mg**
- **IRON: 1.5mg**

ALLERGENS & TIPS

Allergens: Contains almonds - just a heads up!

Tips: Serve with a dollop of Greek yogurt. Cool, right?

GARLIC-SOY MARINATED TURKEY

200 KCAL

2 SERVINGS

15 MIN

INGREDIENTS

- 8 oz (227g) turkey tips
- 2 tbsp (30ml) low-sodium soy sauce
- 1 garlic clove, minced
- 1 tsp (5ml) honey, cuz a bit of sweetness never hurt
- A sprinkle of black pepper
- 1 tsp (5ml) sesame oil (This one's a game-changer!)
- Some chopped green onions for garnish (Trust me on this)

DIRECTIONS

1. Mix soy sauce, garlic, honey, and pepper in a bowl. Dive those turkey tips in.
2. Let them chill and marinate for 10 minutes (sip some tea maybe?).
3. Preheat the air fryer to 375°F (190°C).
4. Drizzle sesame oil over turkey tips.
5. Pop them in the air fryer for 7 minutes.
6. Toss once, fry for another 5-7 minutes.
7. Once golden, sprinkle green onions on top.

NUTRITION

- **CARBS: 8g**
- **PROTEIN: 26g**
- **FAT: 5g**
- **FIBER: 0g**
- **OMEGA 3: 0.1g**
- **VITAMIN D: 0.2µg**
- **CALCIUM: 10mg**
- **IRON: 1mg**

ALLERGENS & TIPS

Allergens: Watch out for soy if you're sensitive.

Tips: Wanna add a zing? A touch of grated ginger in the marinade does wonders!

ROSEMARY ORANGE TURKEY SKEWERS

210 KCAL

2 SERVINGS

20 MIN

INGREDIENTS

- 8 oz (227g) turkey chunks, chill vibes only
- 1 sprig fresh rosemary, coz nature's cool
- 2 tbsp (30ml) orange juice, fresh, not the boxed drama
- 1 tbsp (15ml) orange zest, from the same orange, if possible
- Salt & pepper, just a pinch
- Wooden skewers, soaked in water, they've had their spa day

DIRECTIONS

1. In a bowl, whisk together orange juice, zest, rosemary, salt, and pepper.
2. Add turkey chunks; let them soak up the good vibes for about 10 minutes.
3. Preheat the air fryer to 390°F (200°C).
4. Thread the turkey onto those pre-soaked skewers.
5. Place skewers in the air fryer and cook for 10 minutes.
6. Give them a turn and fry for another 5 minutes.

NUTRITION

- **CARBS: 6g**
- **PROTEIN: 28g**
- **FAT: 4g**
- **FIBER: 1g**
- **OMEGA 3: 0.2g**
- **VITAMIN D: 0.5µg**
- **CALCIUM: 20mg**
- **IRON: 1.2mg**

ALLERGENS & TIPS

Allergens: Contains orange for those citrus-sensitive folks.

Tips: If you're feeling wild, throw in a clove of minced garlic into that marinade.

MEDITERRANEAN SPICED TURKEY THIGHS

220 KCAL

2 SERVINGS

20 MIN

INGREDIENTS

- 2 turkey thighs, about 12 oz (340g) - the meatier, the merrier!
- 1 tbsp (15ml) olive oil - because we're keeping it Mediterranean, right?
- 1 tsp (5g) paprika - for that smoky touch
- 1 tsp (5g) oregano - it's like a mini trip to Greece
- Salt & pepper, as per your taste buds
- 2 garlic cloves, minced (10g) - for that flavor punch

DIRECTIONS

1. Alright, first up, mix olive oil, paprika, oregano, garlic, salt, and pepper in a bowl. Give it a good stir!
2. Slather those turkey thighs with the spiced mix. Make sure they're well-coated.
3. Get that air fryer going to 375°F (190°C).
4. Once it's heated, pop the turkey thighs in.
5. Cook 'em up for about 10 minutes, then flip them over.
6. Another 10 minutes on the other side and voila, you're good to go!

NUTRITION

- **CARBS: 2g**
- **PROTEIN: 30g**
- **FAT: 10g**
- **FIBER: 1g**
- **OMEGA 3: 0.1g**
- **VITAMIN D: 0.5µg**
- **CALCIUM: 20mg**
- **IRON: 2mg**

ALLERGENS & TIPS

Allergens: Watch out for the paprika if you're spice-sensitive.

Tips: Fancy a zesty kick? Squeeze some lemon on top before serving.

TANGY MUSTARD TURKEY DRUMETTES

220 KCAL

2 SERVINGS

20 MIN

INGREDIENTS

- 6 turkey drumettes, roughly 10 oz (280g)
- 1.5 tbsp (23ml) Dijon mustard - the zingy stuff!
- 1 tbsp (15ml) honey - just a touch of sweetness
- 1 tsp (5g) apple cider vinegar - for a lil' kick
- Salt & pepper, your call on the amount
- Dash of olive oil - keeps it slick

DIRECTIONS

1. Whisk together mustard, honey, vinegar, olive oil, salt, and pepper. Kinda fun, right?
2. Coat the drumettes in the tangy goodness. Every nook and cranny, folks!
3. Preheat the air fryer to a cozy 375°F (190°C).
4. Lay the drumettes in there. No crowding, they need space!
5. 10 minutes, then give them a flip.
6. Another 10 and bam, snack time!

NUTRITION

- **CARBS: 8g**
- **PROTEIN: 26g**
- **FAT: 8g**
- **FIBER: 0.2g**
- **OMEGA 3: 0.1g**
- **VITAMIN D: 0.2µg**
- **CALCIUM: 15mg**
- **IRON: 1.5mg**

ALLERGENS & TIPS

Allergens: Heads up for the mustard if you've got a sensitivity.

Tips: A side of celery sticks adds a crunchy contrast. Give it a try!

SMOKY PAPRIKA TURKEY TENDERLOINS

230 KCAL

2 SERVINGS

25 MIN

INGREDIENTS

- 2 turkey tenderloins, about 10 oz (280g) total, 'cause we're keeping it light.
- 1.5 tbsp (23ml) smoked paprika, for that smoky charm.
- 1 tsp (5ml) olive oil, we're not drowning it, just a hint!
- Salt & pepper, you do you.
- A tiny squeeze of lemon juice, for that zesty touch.

DIRECTIONS

1. Rub the tenderloins with smoked paprika, salt, pepper, and that dash of lemon. Trust me, it'll be heavenly.
2. Get that air fryer all warmed up to 375°F (190°C). It's showtime.
3. Drizzle your turkey with olive oil. Stay classy, not greasy.
4. Pop them in the fryer for about 12 minutes.
5. Peek in, flip 'em, and another 8 minutes should do the trick.

NUTRITION

- **CARBS: 2g**
- **PROTEIN: 30g**
- **FAT: 7g**
- **FIBER: 1g**
- **OMEGA 3: 0.2g**
- **VITAMIN D: 0.1µg**
- **CALCIUM: 25mg**
- **IRON: 2mg**

ALLERGENS & TIPS

Allergens: None in this dish, but always double-check your ingredients.

Tips: Throw in a sprinkle of cayenne if you're feeling a lil' spicy!

240 KCAL

2 SERVINGS

20 MIN

PESTO BRUSHED TURKEY SLICES

INGREDIENTS

- 2 turkey slices, 8 oz each (227g)
- 1.5 tbsp (22.5ml) pesto sauce (go light on the oil, alright?)
- A pinch of sea salt, just for that lil' kick
- A smidge of black pepper
- 1 tsp (5ml) olive oil, keeping it heart-healthy!

DIRECTIONS

1. Spread that lush pesto over the turkey slices, and sprinkle on some salt and pepper.
2. Power up your air fryer to 360°F (182°C) – let's get the magic happenin'.
3. Give your turkey a light olive oil massage, but not too much – remember, we're keeping it healthy.
4. Slide them into the fryer, let them groove for about 10 minutes.
5. Time for a quick flip! Another 6 minutes and you're golden.

NUTRITION

- **CARBS: 3g**
- **PROTEIN: 28g**
- **FAT: 9g**
- **FIBER: 1g**
- **OMEGA 3: 0.1g**
- **VITAMIN D: 0.2µg**
- **CALCIUM: 20mg**
- **IRON: 1.5mg**

ALLERGENS & TIPS

Allergens: Contains nuts (from the pesto), but always check your pesto's ingredients..

Tips: Feelin' fancy? Toss some cherry tomatoes in the air fryer during the last 2 minutes

300 KCAL

2 SERVINGS

20 MIN

ALMOND-CRUSTED PORK PATTIES

INGREDIENTS

- 1/2 pound (227g) lean ground pork
- 1/4 cup (30g) crushed almonds
- 1 tsp (5ml) olive oil
- A pinch of salt and pepper
- 1/2 tsp (2.5ml) garlic powder
- A sprig of fresh parsley, finely chopped

DIRECTIONS

1. In a bowl, combine ground pork, garlic powder, parsley, and a pinch of salt and pepper.
2. Shape the mixture into two patties.
3. Lightly coat each patty with olive oil, then press into crushed almonds ensuring both sides are covered.
4. Place patties into the air fryer basket.
5. Cook at 375°F (190°C) for 12 minutes or until cooked through, flipping halfway.

NUTRITION

- **CARBS: 4g**
- **PROTEIN: 26g**
- **FAT: 14g**
- **FIBER: 2g**
- **OMEGA 3: 0.5g**
- **VITAMIN D: 0.2mcg**
- **CALCIUM: 60mg**
- **IRON: 1.2mg**

ALLERGENS & TIPS

Allergens: Contains nuts (almonds); for a zesty kick, add a dash of lemon zest to the patty mix.

Tips: For a zesty kick, add a dash of lemon zest to the patty mix or sprinkle some crushed red pepper flakes for a hint of spice. Giving the patties a quick chill in the fridge before air frying can help them hold their shape better.

BASIL AND GARLIC PORK SKEWERS

275 KCAL

2 SERVINGS

15 MIN

INGREDIENTS

- 1/2 pound (227g) lean pork tenderloin, cut into chunks
- A handful of fresh basil leaves, chopped
- 2 garlic cloves, minced
- 1 tsp (5ml) olive oil
- A sprinkle of salt and pepper
- 4 wooden skewers, soaked in water

DIRECTIONS

1. In your favorite mixing bowl, toss together the pork chunks, minced garlic, chopped basil, olive oil, and your salt & pepper.
2. Thread those flavorful pork chunks onto the soaked skewers.
3. Pop 'em into the air fryer basket.
4. Cook at 370°F (188°C) for about 10 minutes, turning once, until they're golden and perfectly cooked.

NUTRITION

- **CARBS: 2g**
- **PROTEIN: 25g**
- **FAT: 9g**
- **FIBER: 1g**
- **OMEGA 3: 0.3g**
- **VITAMIN D: 0.1mcg**
- **CALCIUM: 25mg**
- **IRON: 1.4mg**

ALLERGENS & TIPS

Allergens: This dish contains pork which can be an allergen for some, and garlic which may cause reactions for those with FODMAP sensitivities.

Tips: Remember, soaking skewers in water helps avoid burning, and for an extra twist, toss in some lemon zest with the marinade!

26

SPICED TURMERIC PORK MEDALLIONS

260 KCAL

2 SERVINGS

20 MIN

INGREDIENTS

- 1/2 pound (227g) lean pork tenderloin, sliced into medallions
- 1 tsp (5ml) turmeric powder
- 1/2 tsp (2.5ml) paprika
- A hint of black pepper
- 1 tsp (5ml) olive oil
- A smidge of salt

DIRECTIONS

1. Lay out your pork medallions and season them generously with turmeric, paprika, salt, and pepper.
2. Lightly drizzle the medallions with olive oil to coat.
3. Neatly arrange them in the air fryer basket.
4. Cook at 375°F (190°C) for 10-12 minutes, turning midway, until they're tender and beautifully golden.

NUTRITION

- **CARBS: 1g**
- **PROTEIN: 24g**
- **FAT: 7g**
- **FIBER: 0.5g**
- **OMEGA 3: 0.2g**
- **VITAMIN D: 0.1mcg**
- **CALCIUM: 20mg**
- **IRON: 1.6mg**

ALLERGENS & TIPS

Allergens: This recipe contains pork which can be a common allergen. Turmeric, while offering many health benefits, can sometimes cause stomach upsets in sensitive individuals.

Tips: Jazz up the dish with a spritz of lime before serving, and resting the medallions for a few minutes post-cooking enhances tenderness.

27

300 KCAL

2 SERVINGS

35 MIN

LEMON-THYME INFUSED PORK RIBS

INGREDIENTS

- 1/2 pound (227g) pork ribs, preferably lean
- 1 lemon, zest and juice
- 2 sprigs fresh thyme (or 1 tsp dried thyme if you're in a pinch)
- 1 tbsp (15ml) olive oil (you know, the good kind)
- Salt and pepper to taste (life's too short for bland food)

NUTRITION

- **CARBS: 5g**
- **PROTEIN: 28g**
- **FAT: 16g**
- **FIBER: 1g**
- **OMEGA 3: 0.1g**
- **VITAMIN D: 0.5mcg**
- **CALCIUM: 50mg**
- **IRON: 1.2mg**

DIRECTIONS

1. Mix that lemon zest, juice, thyme, olive oil, salt, and pepper in a bowl. Make sure it's all friendly in there.
2. Rub this zesty mix all over your ribs. Let them chill in the fridge for about 10 minutes (it's like a mini spa day for them).
3. Preheat your air fryer to 360°F (180°C).
4. Once ready, toss those ribs in. Cook for about 20 minutes. Remember to flip them halfway!

ALLERGENS & TIPS

Allergens: This recipe obviously contains pork. Some people might react to citric acid in lemons, so be aware if you're sensitive. And for those herb aficionados, fresh thyme can occasionally cause skin reactions for some.

Tips: If you've got a herb garden, fresh thyme really amps up the flavor. Also, ribs are even better when served with a fresh salad on the side!

GARLIC-SOY MARINATED PORK TIPS

280 KCAL

2 SERVINGS

30 MIN

INGREDIENTS

- 1/2 pound (227g) lean pork tips
- 3 garlic cloves, minced
- 2 tbsp (30ml) low-sodium soy sauce
- 1 tbsp (15ml) olive oil
- 1/2 tsp black pepper
- A pinch of red pepper flakes (optional)

NUTRITION

- **CARBS: 4g**
- **PROTEIN: 30g**
- **FAT: 12g**
- **FIBER: 0.3g**
- **OMEGA 3: 0.2g**
- **VITAMIN D: 1mcg**
- **CALCIUM: 20mg**
- **IRON: 1.8mg**

DIRECTIONS

1. In a bowl, whisk together minced garlic, soy sauce, olive oil, black pepper, and red pepper flakes.
2. Toss in the pork tips, ensuring they're well coated.
3. Let them sit and soak up those flavors for about 10 minutes.
4. Preheat the air fryer to 375°F (190°C).
5. Place the marinated pork tips in the fryer and cook for 18 minutes. Give them a stir midway.

ALLERGENS & TIPS

Allergens: This dish contains soy and garlic; both can be allergens for some.

Tips: To elevate the dish, consider adding a dash of honey for a sweet twist.

TANGY ORANGE PORK SKEWERS

270 KCAL

2 SERVINGS

30 MIN

INGREDIENTS

- 1/2 pound (227g) lean pork, cut into cubes
- Juice of 1 orange (around 1/4 cup or 60ml)
- Zest from half an orange
- 1 tbsp (15ml) low-sodium soy sauce
- 1/2 tsp (2.5ml) honey
- 2 small green onions, chopped
- A sprinkle of salt and pepper

DIRECTIONS

1. Alright, first off, mix together the orange juice, zest, soy sauce, honey, and half of the green onions in a bowl. You're making a killer marinade here!
2. Add those pork cubes to the bowl. Let them swim and chill in that tangy mix for about 10 minutes.
3. Time to prep the air fryer! Crank it up to 390°F (200°C).
4. Skewer the pork cubes, then pop them into the air fryer.
5. Let them sizzle and dance for 14 minutes, turning halfway for an even cook.

NUTRITION

- **CARBS: 5g**
- **PROTEIN: 28g**
- **FAT: 9g**
- **FIBER: 0.5g**
- **OMEGA 3: 0.2g**
- **VITAMIN D: 0.8mcg**
- **CALCIUM: 28mg**
- **IRON: 1.5mg**

ALLERGENS & TIPS

Allergens: Keep an eye out if you're sensitive to soy.

Tips: For a fun twist, throw in some bell pepper chunks between the pork on the skewers.

30

SESAME GINGER PORK BALLS

210 KCAL

2 SERVINGS

25 MIN

INGREDIENTS

- 1/2 pound (227g) lean pork mince
- 1 tsp (5ml) fresh ginger, grated
- 1 tbsp (15ml) sesame oil
- 1 tbsp (15ml) low-sodium soy sauce
- 1/2 tbsp (7.5ml) sesame seeds
- A pinch of black pepper
- 2 tsp (10ml) chopped fresh parsley

NUTRITION

- **CARBS: 2g**
- **PROTEIN: 24g**
- **FAT: 12g**
- **FIBER: 0.7g**
- **OMEGA 3: 0.3g**
- **VITAMIN D: 1mcg**
- **CALCIUM: 35mg**
- **IRON: 1.4mg**

DIRECTIONS

1. Get a bowl and mix that pork mince, ginger, half the sesame oil, and soy sauce.
2. Shape this mix into small balls. Size them up just right for a bite or two.
3. Drizzle the remaining sesame oil over your balls and sprinkle them with sesame seeds.
4. Pop those beauties in the air fryer at 375°F (190°C).
5. After 12 minutes or when they're golden brown, take them out. Sprinkle with parsley.

ALLERGENS & TIPS

Allergens: Watch out if you're dodging soy and sesame – this recipe's got both.

Tips: For extra flair, consider a squeeze of lime. Oh, and those sesame seeds? Toast them beforehand for an elevated nutty flavor. Remember, fresh ginger always beats the powdered stuff!

BALSAMIC GLAZED BEEF RIBBONS

320 KCAL

2 SERVINGS

3 MIN

INGREDIENTS

- 8oz (227g) beef ribbons, thinly sliced
- 3 tbsp (45 ml) balsamic vinegar
- 1 tbsp (15 ml) honey
- 1 clove garlic, minced
- ½ tsp (2.5 ml) rosemary, finely chopped
- Salt and pepper, to taste
- 1 tbsp (15 ml) olive oil

DIRECTIONS

1. In a bowl, whisk together balsamic vinegar, honey, garlic, rosemary, salt, and pepper.
2. Toss beef ribbons in the mixture until well-coated.
3. Preheat the air fryer to 375°F (190°C).
4. Lay beef ribbons in a single layer in the air fryer. Cook for 8-10 minutes, flipping halfway.
5. Remove, let rest for 2 minutes, and serve!

NUTRITION

- **CARBS: 15g**
- **PROTEIN: 22g**
- **FAT: 10g**
- **FIBER: 1g**
- **OMEGA 3: 0.2g**
- **VITAMIN D: 1.2µg**
- **CALCIUM: 18mg**
- **IRON: 2.5mg**

ALLERGENS & TIPS

Allergens: This dish contains potential allergens like honey.

Tips: For an extra kick, consider adding a pinch of chili flakes or swap honey with maple syrup for a subtle sweetness.

SPICED TURMERIC BEEF MEDALLIONS

230 KCAL

2 SERVINGS

25 MIN

INGREDIENTS

- 8oz (227g) beef medallions
- 1 tsp (5 ml) ground turmeric
- ½ tsp (2.5 ml) paprika
- 1 tbsp (15 ml) olive oil
- Salt and pepper, for seasoning
- 1 garlic clove, minced
- Zest of ½ lemon

NUTRITION

- **CARBS: 4g**
- **PROTEIN: 26g**
- **FAT: 9g**
- **FIBER: 1g**
- **OMEGA 3: 0.1g**
- **VITAMIN D: 1µg**
- **CALCIUM: 20mg**
- **IRON: 2.8mg**

DIRECTIONS

1. Combine that golden turmeric, paprika, olive oil, salt, pepper, garlic, and lemon zest in a bowl.
2. Rub this zesty mix all over the beef medallions. Let them chill for about 5 minutes, soaking up those flavors.
3. Now, fire up that air fryer of yours to 375°F (190°C).
4. Lay the beef medallions in it, making sure they aren't overcrowded.
5. Cook them for about 12 minutes, giving them a gentle flip halfway.
6. Once done, let 'em rest for 2 minutes before you dig in!

ALLERGENS & TIPS

Allergens: Contains potential allergens: beef and garlic. Caution with turmeric—it stains!

Tips: This dish has potential allergens like garlic. Jazz it up with fresh herbs or serve over a salad for added freshness.

210 KCAL

2 SERVINGS

25 MIN

TANGY ORANGE-ZEST BEEF SKEWERS

INGREDIENTS

- 8oz (227g) beef cubes
- Zest of 1 orange
- 1 tbsp (15 ml) low-sodium soy sauce
- ½ tbsp (7.5 ml) honey
- 1 garlic clove, finely chopped
- Pinch of chili flakes
- Salt to taste

DIRECTIONS

1. In a mixing bowl, combine orange zest, soy sauce, honey, garlic, chili flakes, and salt.
2. Toss in the beef cubes ensuring they are well-coated.
3. Let them sit for about 10 minutes to marinate.
4. Preheat your air fryer to 375°F (190°C).
5. Thread beef cubes onto skewers.
6. Place skewers in the air fryer, cooking for 15 minutes, turning halfway through.

NUTRITION

- **CARBS: 7g**
- **PROTEIN: 27g**
- **FAT: 7g**
- **FIBER: 0.8g**
- **OMEGA 3: 0.1g**
- **VITAMIN D: 0.9µg**
- **CALCIUM: 18mg**
- **IRON: 2.6mg**

ALLERGENS & TIPS

Allergens: Watch out for beef, soy, and garlic if you have allergies.

Tips: To infuse even more flavor, marinate beef overnight in the fridge.

34

HONEY-SRIRACHA BEEF NUGGETS

205 KCAL

2 SERVINGS

25 MIN

INGREDIENTS

- 8oz (227g) beef, cut into bite-sized pieces
- 1 tbsp (15 ml) honey
- 1 tsp (5 ml) sriracha sauce (add more if you like it spicy!)
- A pinch of salt
- ½ tsp (2.5 ml) olive oil

DIRECTIONS

1. Whisk together honey, sriracha sauce, olive oil, and salt in a bowl.
2. Toss in the beef pieces making sure they get all that yummy coating.
3. Let 'em rest for 5 minutes.
4. Preheat your trusty air fryer to 380°F (193°C).
5. Pop the beef nuggets in and let them sizzle for 12 minutes, giving them a little shake halfway.

NUTRITION

- **CARBS: 8g**
- **PROTEIN: 26g**
- **FAT: 5g**
- **FIBER: 0.2g**
- **OMEGA 3: 0.1g**
- **VITAMIN D: 0.7µg**
- **CALCIUM: 15mg**
- **IRON: 2.5mg**

ALLERGENS & TIPS

Allergens: Got allergies? Check for honey, beef, and sriracha.

Tips: For an extra kick, add a sprinkle of crushed red pepper to the marinade!

CUMIN-SPICED BEEF PATTIES

210 KCAL

2 SERVINGS

20 MIN

INGREDIENTS

- 8oz (227g) lean ground beef
- 1 tsp (5 ml) cumin powder
- 1 garlic clove, finely chopped
- Salt and pepper to taste
- ½ tsp (2.5 ml) olive oil for brushing

DIRECTIONS

1. In a bowl, combine beef, cumin, garlic, salt, and pepper.
2. Form the mixture into two even patties.
3. Brush each patty lightly with olive oil.
4. Heat the air fryer to 375°F (190°C).
5. Place patties in the fryer and cook for 8 minutes, flipping halfway through, until golden brown and cooked to your liking.

NUTRITION

- **CARBS: 2g**
- **PROTEIN: 25g**
- **FAT: 9g**
- **FIBER: 0.1g**
- **OMEGA 3: 0.2g**
- **VITAMIN D: 1.5µg**
- **CALCIUM: 10mg**
- **IRON: 2.8mg**

ALLERGENS & TIPS

Allergens: Got Chicken & Garlic in here, heads up! And sometimes, broths have hidden surprises, so always double-check.

Tips: A slice of multi-grain bread complements this stew perfectly. Also, organically sourced chicken just feels right, doesn't it? And for a twist, a bay leaf wouldn't hurt!

GARLIC-HERB INFUSED BEEF RIBS

215 KCAL

2 SERVINGS

20 MIN

INGREDIENTS

- 8oz (227g) beef ribs (choose the leanest ones you can find)
- 2 garlic cloves, minced (because garlic is life)
- 1 tbsp (15ml) mixed dried herbs (basil, rosemary, oregano, your pick!)
- A pinch of salt and pepper, for that zing!
- ½ tsp (2.5 ml) olive oil, just a drizzle

DIRECTIONS

1. Grab a bowl and toss in the beef ribs, garlic, herbs, salt, and pepper. Give them a good mix.
2. Drizzle them with that olive oil, making sure they're well coated.
3. Fire up your air fryer to 375°F (190°C).
4. Gently place those ribs in, letting them sizzle and cook for 10 minutes. Halfway through, give them a flip!

NUTRITION

- **CARBS: 3g**
- **PROTEIN: 26g**
- **FAT: 10g**
- **FIBER: 0.5g**
- **OMEGA 3: 0.4g**
- **VITAMIN D: 1µg**
- **CALCIUM: 12mg**
- **IRON: 3mg**

ALLERGENS & TIPS

Allergens: Allergy heads up: contains beef and garlic.

Tips: Serve with a lemon wedge to cut through the richness.

MAPLE-MUSTARD BEEF BITES

210 KCAL

2 SERVINGS

20 MIN

INGREDIENTS

- Beef chunks, lean: 8oz (227g)
- Pure maple syrup: 1 tbsp (15ml)
- Whole grain mustard: 1 tbsp (15ml)
- Olive oil: ½ tsp (2.5ml)
- Salt & pepper: a pinch each

DIRECTIONS

1. Mix maple syrup, mustard, salt, and pepper in a bowl.
2. Add beef chunks and ensure they're well-coated.
3. Preheat your air fryer to 375°F (190°C).
4. Lightly coat beef with olive oil and air-fry for 8 minutes, turning once.

NUTRITION

- **CARBS: 8g**
- **PROTEIN: 25g**
- **FAT: 9g**
- **FIBER: 0.6g**
- **OMEGA 3: 0.2g**
- **VITAMIN D: 0.5µg**
- **CALCIUM: 18mg**
- **IRON: 2mg**

ALLERGENS & TIPS

Allergens: This dish contains beef and mustard.

Tips: Keep leftovers in an airtight container, and they taste amazing chilled!

CUMIN-SPICED LAMB MEDALLIONS

250 KCAL

2 SERVINGS

15 MIN

INGREDIENTS

- 4 juicy lamb medallions (6 oz/170g each)
- A touch of cumin powder (1 tsp/5g)
- Salt and pepper (however much feels right)
- A drizzle of olive oil (1 tbsp/15ml)
- Some lemon juice for zing

DIRECTIONS

1. Grab those lamb medallions and shower them in cumin, salt, and pepper.
2. Give them a light olive oil massage.
3. Slide them into the air fryer, 400°F (200°C). Around 8 minutes should get them perfectly cooked, but don't forget that halfway flip.
4. When they're all crispy and tempting, hit them with that lemon juice.
5. Plate, devour, repeat!

NUTRITION

- **CARBS: 0.5g**
- **PROTEIN: 25g**
- **FAT: 8g**
- **FIBER: 0.2g**
- **OMEGA 3: 0.1g**
- **VITAMIN D: 0.5mcg**
- **CALCIUM: 20mg**
- **IRON: 2mg**

ALLERGENS & TIPS

Allergens: For those who might wonder, this dish contains cumin and lamb, so it might be a good idea to check for sensitivities.

Tips: While prepping, if you're feeling a bit adventurous, mix in some lemon zest with the cumin rub; it just elevates the flavor to another level.

SMOKY PAPRIKA LAMB RIBLETS

230 KCAL

2 SERVINGS

10 MIN

INGREDIENTS

- 6 tender lamb riblets (8 oz/225g in total)
- 1 relaxed dash of smoky paprika (1.5 tsp/7.5g)
- Season with salt and pepper (to taste)
- 1 chill splash of olive oil (1/2 tbsp/7.5ml)
- Some squeezed lemon for a fresh end note (1 tbsp/15ml)

DIRECTIONS

1. Lay the riblets out, give them a good dusting of smoky paprika, salt, and pepper.
2. Drizzle them with olive oil, ensuring they're all glossed up.
3. Pop them into the air fryer at 375°F (190°C) for about 7 minutes, giving them a flip at the halfway mark.
4. Once they're crisped to perfection, add a splash of lemon juice for a bright finish.

NUTRITION

- **CARBS: 0.3g**
- **PROTEIN: 24g**
- **FAT: 7g**
- **FIBER: 0.1g**
- **OMEGA 3: 0.1g**
- **VITAMIN D: 0.4mcg**
- **CALCIUM: 18mg**
- **IRON: 1.8mg**

ALLERGENS & TIPS

Allergens: Keep in mind this dish contains lamb (for those sensitive or allergic to certain meats) and smoky paprika which might be a concern for some spice allergens.

Tips: Feel free to swap the lemon for a hint of lime for a tangy twist or add some herbs like rosemary for a deeper flavor profile.

ZESTY LEMON-PEPPER LAMB BITES

240 KCAL

2 SERVINGS

10 MIN

INGREDIENTS

- 8 pieces of juicy lamb bites (10 oz/280g)
- A nice sprinkle of that tangy lemon zest (1 lemon/14g)
- Generous shakes of black pepper (1 tsp/5g)
- A little pinch of salt, just right (to taste)
- Let's not forget, a light drizzle of olive oil (1/2 tbsp/7.5ml)

NUTRITION

- **CARBS: 0.5g**
- **PROTEIN: 26g**
- **FAT: 8g**
- **FIBER: 0.2g**
- **OMEGA 3: 0.2g**
- **VITAMIN D: 0.6mcg**
- **CALCIUM: 20mg**
- **IRON: 2mg**

DIRECTIONS

1. Grab those lamb bites, and rub them up with your lemon zest, black pepper, and salt. Get them all coated and fragrant.
2. Now, before they hop into the air fryer, give them a little olive oil shine.
3. Alright, into the air fryer they go at 390°F (200°C) for about 8 minutes. Halfway through, give 'em a little flip for even crispiness.

ALLERGENS & TIPS

Allergens: Hey there, this dish has lamb, so if you're sensitive to certain meats, take note. And, for the zesty fans, the lemon used could be a concern for some citrus allergies.

Tips: Switch up the game! Maybe try orange zest or add a sprinkle of dried herbs like oregano or thyme, which might give a whole new spin on flavors.

TERIYAKI-GLAZED LAMB SKEWERS

230 KCAL

2 SERVINGS

15 MIN

INGREDIENTS

- Lamb cubes, nice and lean (12 oz/340g)
- A smidge of olive oil for light coating (1/2 tbsp/7.5ml)
- Salt to keep things balanced (to taste)
- Store-bought or homemade teriyaki sauce, low-sodium (3 tbsp/45ml)
- Bamboo skewers, soaked in water

NUTRITION

- **CARBS: 15g**
- **PROTEIN: 28g**
- **FAT: 7g**
- **FIBER: 0g**
- **OMEGA 3: 0.3g**
- **VITAMIN D: 1mcg**
- **CALCIUM: 22mg**
- **IRON: 2.5mg**

DIRECTIONS

1. First things first, get those lamb cubes threaded onto your skewers. Don't crowd them; give them some space.
2. Lightly brush them with olive oil. Season with salt, not too much though.
3. Get that air fryer going at 400°F (205°C). Place skewers in and cook for about 7 minutes.
4. While they're doing their thing, warm up your teriyaki sauce. Once the skewers are done, brush them generously.
5. Pop them back into the fryer for another 2 minutes to get that glaze going.

ALLERGENS & TIPS

Allergens: Just a quick heads up - for those with allergies, this dish contains lamb and possibly gluten or soy from the teriyaki sauce, so please ensure you're using a suitable one if needed.

Tips: While store-bought is handy, making your own teriyaki can reduce added sugars. Also, you can toss on some sesame seeds or chopped scallions to amp up the flair.

HERB-CRUSTED LAMB STEAKS

260 KCAL

2 SERVINGS

20 MIN

INGREDIENTS

- Some tender lamb steaks (12 oz/340g)
- Tiny bit of olive oil (1/2 tbsp/7.5ml)
- Salt, just a sprinkle (to taste)
- Some mixed dried herbs (think rosemary, thyme, and oregano) (2 tsp/10ml)
- A clove of garlic, finely chopped

NUTRITION

- **CARBS: 2g**
- **PROTEIN: 30g**
- **FAT: 14g**
- **FIBER: 0.5g**
- **OMEGA 3: 0.4g**
- **VITAMIN D: 1.2mcg**
- **CALCIUM: 15mg**
- **IRON: 3mg**

DIRECTIONS

1. Rub those lamb steaks with garlic. It's all about the flavor!
2. Mix olive oil, salt, and your chosen herbs in a bowl. Give it a good stir.
3. Slather that herb mix onto the lamb. Both sides, okay?
4. Crank up your air fryer to 400°F (205°C). In go the steaks for about 8 minutes. Midway, turn them for an even cook.
5. When they're golden and smelling oh-so-good, pull them out. Let them rest for a few.

ALLERGENS & TIPS

Allergens: Hey, just a quick word to the wise: this recipe includes lamb and can have garlic, which some folks might be allergic to, so just keep an eye out.

Tips: If you're aiming for extra juicy steaks, consider marinating them for an hour or so before cooking. And remember, always let meat rest before digging in; it keeps it tender!

SESAME GINGER LAMB BALLS

280 KCAL

2 SERVINGS

25 MIN

INGREDIENTS

- Tender lamb ground (8 oz/227g)
- White sesame seeds for that crunch (1 tbsp/15ml)
- Fresh ginger, finely grated (1 tsp/5ml)
- Dash of low-sodium soy sauce (1 tbsp/15ml)
- Little green onions, sliced (1/2 cup/120ml)
- Few sprigs of fresh coriander, chopped

NUTRITION

- **CARBS: 4g**
- **PROTEIN: 26g**
- **FAT: 18g**
- **FIBER: 1g**
- **OMEGA 3: 0.2g**
- **VITAMIN D: 1.0mcg**
- **CALCIUM: 20mg**
- **IRON: 2.5mg**

DIRECTIONS

1. In a mixing bowl, combine the lamb with ginger, soy sauce, half the green onions, and coriander.
2. Roll the mixture into small balls. You should get around 6-8.
3. Lightly press sesame seeds onto each ball.
4. Preheat your air fryer at 375°F (190°C).
5. Place the lamb balls in the air fryer and cook for about 12 minutes or until well-done.
6. Once out, sprinkle the remaining green onions over the top.

ALLERGENS & TIPS

Allergens: This recipe features lamb, sesame seeds, and soy sauce. Some individuals can be sensitive to sesame or soy, so it's worth noting for guests.

Tips: For an even bolder flavor, consider letting the lamb marinate in the ginger-soy mixture for about 30 minutes before cooking.

SPICY HARISSA LAMB STRIPS

260 KCAL

2 SERVINGS

20 MIN

INGREDIENTS

- Lean lamb strips: 8 oz/227g
- Harissa paste: 1 tbsp/15ml
- 1 Lime (zested and juiced)
- Salt: to taste
- Olive oil: 1 tsp/5ml

DIRECTIONS

1. First things first, mix the harissa paste, lime zest, lime juice, and salt in a bowl.
2. Toss in the lamb strips, ensuring they get a good coat.
3. Let them sit and soak up the flavors for about 10 minutes.
4. Drizzle that little bit of olive oil over the strips.
5. Fire up your air fryer to 375°F (190°C) and toss those lamb strips in.
6. Cook for about 8-10 minutes, flipping halfway through. We want them browned but still juicy inside.

NUTRITION

- **CARBS: 2g**
- **PROTEIN: 29g**
- **FAT: 12g**
- **FIBER: 1g**
- **OMEGA 3: 0.3g**
- **VITAMIN D: 1.2mcg**
- **CALCIUM: 28mg**
- **IRON: 3.1mg**

ALLERGENS & TIPS

Allergens: Watch out if you're sensitive to spices from the harissa paste, and for anyone with lamb allergies. Also, always check the harissa paste ingredients; sometimes they throw in unexpected stuff!

Tips: Trust me, you might want to marinate these strips overnight. It makes a world of difference in flavor. And if you're not a spice lover, dial back on the harissa.

GARLIC-PARSLEY SCALLOPS

220 KCAL

2 SERVINGS

15 MIN

INGREDIENTS

- Fresh scallops: 8 oz/227g
- Garlic cloves (minced): 2
- Fresh parsley (chopped): 1/4 cup (60ml)
- Olive oil: 1 tbsp/15ml
- Lemon juice: 1 tbsp/15ml
- Salt: 1/8 tsp
- Black pepper: 1/8 tsp

DIRECTIONS

1. Hey there! First, make sure you rinse those scallops and pat them dry. Nobody likes a watery scallop.
2. Alright, grab a bowl and mix garlic, parsley, olive oil, lemon juice, salt, and pepper. Give it a good mix.
3. Toss those scallops into the marinade, ensuring they're all nice and coated.
4. Let those babies sit for about 5 minutes.
5. Time to heat the air fryer. Get it going at 400°F (204°C).
6. Once ready, pop the scallops in and cook for 6-8 minutes, until they're golden and tender.

NUTRITION

- **CARBS: 5g**
- **PROTEIN: 20g**
- **FAT: 8g**
- **FIBER: 0.5g**
- **OMEGA 3: 0.7g**
- **VITAMIN D: 2mcg**
- **CALCIUM: 20mg**
- **IRON: 1mg**

ALLERGENS & TIPS

Allergens: Hey folks, be aware that this recipe contains scallops, which are shellfish. People with shellfish allergies or sensitivities should steer clear.

Tips: Wanna get fancy? Serve these on a bed of mixed greens with a light lemon dressing. Also, always make sure your scallops are fresh; it makes a world of a difference in flavor and texture!

BASIL-PESTO MARINATED SWORDFISH CHUNKS

215 KCAL

2 SERVINGS

20 MIN

INGREDIENTS

- Swordfish steaks (cut into 1-inch chunks): 7 oz (200g)
- Basil-pesto: 2 tbsp (30ml)
- Lemon zest: 1 tsp
- Lemon juice: 1 tbsp (15ml)
- Olive oil: 1/2 tbsp (7.5ml)
- Salt: 1/4 tsp
- Black pepper: 1/4 tsp

NUTRITION

- **CARBS: 3g**
- **PROTEIN: 25g**
- **FAT: 8g**
- **FIBER: 1g**
- **OMEGA 3: 1.2g**
- **VITAMIN D: 2.5mcg**
- **CALCIUM: 22mg**
- **IRON: 0.7mg**

DIRECTIONS

1. In a mixing bowl, combine basil-pesto, lemon zest, lemon juice, olive oil, salt, and pepper. Mix it up.
2. Add in the swordfish chunks and ensure they're well-coated with the marinade.
3. Allow it to marinate for about 10 minutes.
4. Preheat your air fryer to 375°F (190°C).
5. Arrange the swordfish chunks in the air fryer, ensuring they're not overlapping.
6. Cook for 8-10 minutes, or until they're golden and cooked through.

ALLERGENS & TIPS

Allergens: This recipe contains swordfish, which some might be allergic to, so be cautious if you have any fish sensitivities or allergies.

Tips: Pairing this dish with a fresh salad enhances the meal. Remember, marinating for longer (up to 30 minutes) can provide a deeper flavor. Enjoy!

BALSAMIC-GLAZED SQUID RIBBONS

190 KCAL

2 SERVINGS

15 MIN

INGREDIENTS

- Fresh squid tubes, sliced into ribbons: 8 oz (230g)
- Balsamic vinegar: 3 tbsp (45ml)
- Honey: 1 tbsp (15ml)
- Olive oil: 1/2 tbsp (7.5ml)
- Red pepper flakes: a pinch
- Salt: 1/4 tsp
- Black pepper: 1/4 tsp

NUTRITION

- **CARBS: 12g**
- **PROTEIN: 18g**
- **FAT: 5g**
- **FIBER: 0g**
- **OMEGA 3: 0.5g**
- **VITAMIN D: 2mcg**
- **CALCIUM: 30mg**
- **IRON: 1mg**

DIRECTIONS

1. Let's start by whisking together balsamic vinegar, honey, olive oil, red pepper flakes, salt, and pepper in a bowl. This will be our zesty glaze.
2. Toss those lovely squid ribbons into the glaze, ensuring they're well covered.
3. Chill out and let them marinate for about 10 minutes, it's worth the wait.
4. Heat up your trusty air fryer to 375°F (190°C).
5. Arrange the squid ribbons without crowding. We want them to cook evenly, right?
6. Air-fry for 5-7 minutes. Keep an eye out, so they don't overcook.

ALLERGENS & TIPS

Allergens: Heads up, folks! This recipe has squid (obviously). If you've got seafood allergies, you'll want to steer clear of this dish.

Tips: For a richer flavor, let the squid marinate longer, but never overcook them. They turn rubbery super quick, so keep an eye out!

160 KCAL

2 SERVINGS

20 MIN

ZESTY ORANGE-ZEST CRAB CAKES

INGREDIENTS

- Lump crab meat: 6 oz (170g)
- Orange zest: 1 tsp (5ml)
- Bread crumbs, whole grain: 1/4 cup (30g)
- Egg white: 1
- Green onions, finely chopped: 2 tbsp (30ml)
- Mayonnaise, low-fat: 1 tbsp (15ml)
- Dijon mustard: 1/2 tsp (2.5ml)
- Salt and pepper to taste

NUTRITION

- **CARBS: 14g**
- **PROTEIN: 15g**
- **FAT: 4g**
- **FIBER: 2g**
- **OMEGA 3: 0.6g**
- **VITAMIN D: 9.7mcg**
- **CALCIUM: 47mg**
- **IRON: 0.7mg**

DIRECTIONS

1. Mix crab meat, orange zest, bread crumbs, egg white, green onions, mayonnaise, Dijon mustard, salt, and pepper in a bowl.
2. Form into two even cakes.
3. Preheat air fryer to 375°F (190°C).
4. Gently place crab cakes in the fryer and cook for 12 minutes or until golden brown, turning once halfway.

ALLERGENS & TIPS

Allergens: This dish features crab, so those allergic to shellfish should take note and opt for something else. Always better to be safe!

Tips: Use fresh orange zest for the brightest flavor and don't overmix; keeping the crab lumps intact makes for a better texture in the cakes.

SMOKY BBQ OCTOPUS LEGS

135 KCAL

2 SERVINGS

25 MIN

INGREDIENTS

- Octopus legs: 4 (about 8oz / 227g)
- Low-fat BBQ sauce: 3 tbsp (45ml)
- Smoked paprika: 1/2 tsp (2.5ml)
- Lemon zest: 1/4 tsp (1.25ml)
- Olive oil, extra virgin: 1/2 tbsp (7.5ml)
- Fresh thyme: 1/2 tsp (2.5ml)
- Salt and pepper: Just a sprinkle

NUTRITION

- **CARBS: 8g**
- **PROTEIN: 18g**
- **FAT: 2g**
- **FIBER: 1g**
- **OMEGA 3: 0.4g**
- **VITAMIN D: 8mcg**
- **CALCIUM: 60mg**
- **IRON: 3mg**

DIRECTIONS

1. First, combine your BBQ sauce, smoked paprika, lemon zest, olive oil, and thyme. Give it a good mix.
2. Time to treat those octopus legs! Coat them generously with the mixture.
3. Fire up your air fryer to 380°F (193°C).
4. Arrange those sauced-up legs in the basket and let them cook for about 15 minutes or until they've got a nice char to them. You're looking for that crispy edge!

ALLERGENS & TIPS

Allergens: Just so you know, this recipe contains seafood, specifically octopus. Always double-check for any allergies, especially if seafood has been a tricky one for you or your guests in the past.

Tips: When it comes to octopus, freshness is key! Also, pre-cooking the legs in boiling water for about 5 minutes can make them super tender post-air frying. Enjoy and happy cooking!

50

HONEY-MUSTARD HALIBUT FILLETS

180 KCAL

2 SERVINGS

20 MIN

INGREDIENTS

- Halibut fillets: 2 (6oz each / 170g each)
- Raw honey: 1 tbsp (15ml)
- Dijon mustard: 1.5 tbsp (22.5ml)
- Olive oil: 1 tsp (5ml)
- Lemon juice: 2 tsp (10ml)
- Fresh parsley, chopped: 1 tbsp (15ml)
- Salt: 1/4 tsp (1.25ml)
- Black pepper: 1/8 tsp (0.6ml)

DIRECTIONS

1. In a bowl, whisk honey, Dijon mustard, olive oil, and lemon juice.
2. Season the halibut fillets with salt and pepper.
3. Apply the honey-mustard mixture generously over each fillet.
4. Set the air fryer to 375°F (190°C).
5. Place the seasoned fillets into the air fryer basket and cook for 12-14 minutes, or until fish is flaky.
6. Sprinkle with fresh parsley before serving.

NUTRITION

- **CARBS: 7g**
- **PROTEIN: 25g**
- **FAT: 3g**
- **FIBER: 0g**
- **OMEGA 3: 1g**
- **VITAMIN D: 4.5mcg**
- **CALCIUM: 15mg**
- **IRON: 0.5mg**

ALLERGENS & TIPS

Allergens: This recipe has fish, specifically halibut, and mustard. Those with seafood or mustard allergies should steer clear or seek alternatives.

Tips: The skin can be left on or removed based on preference, but remember, a lot of flavors can be found in the skin! And always check the fillet's thickness, as it can alter the cooking time.

CUMIN-SPICED TROUT MEDALLIONS

185 KCAL

2 SERVINGS

15 MIN

INGREDIENTS

- Fresh trout medallions: 2 (5oz each / 142g each)
- Ground cumin: 1 tsp (5ml)
- Ground turmeric: 1/4 tsp (1.25ml)
- Olive oil: 1/2 tsp (2.5ml)
- Lemon zest: 1/2 tsp (2.5ml)
- Fresh cilantro, chopped: 1 tbsp (15ml)
- Salt & pepper: just a pinch of each!

DIRECTIONS

1. Let's start by mixing that cumin, turmeric, olive oil, and lemon zest in a bowl. It's gonna be our flavor-packed marinade.
2. Rub that awesome mix on both sides of our trout medallions.
3. Set your air fryer to 360°F (182°C), alright?
4. Toss in those seasoned trout pieces and let them cook for about 8-10 minutes. We're looking for a golden-brown finish.
5. Sprinkle some fresh cilantro when it's done. Trust me, it adds a punch!

NUTRITION

- **CARBS: 0g**
- **PROTEIN: 22g**
- **FAT: 8g**
- **FIBER: 0g**
- **OMEGA 3: 1.8g**
- **VITAMIN D: 4.2mcg**
- **CALCIUM: 30mg**
- **IRON: 1.4mg**

ALLERGENS & TIPS

Allergens: Heads up, mates! This dish has fish, particularly trout, so anyone with seafood allergies might want to consider alternatives or maybe just skip this one.

Tips: Go on, play around with the herbs - maybe some fresh mint or parsley. Remember, trout's delicate, so keep an eye on it to avoid overcooking.

CRISPY PLANTAIN CHIPS

110 KCAL

2 SERVINGS

10 MIN

INGREDIENTS

- Green plantains: 2 medium-sized (6oz / 170g each)
- Olive oil: 1 tsp (5ml)
- Sea salt: a pinch or two
- Optional: Paprika or chili powder for a dash of heat!

DIRECTIONS

1. Peel plantains and slice them thinly, about 1/8 inch (0.3cm) thick.
2. Drizzle with olive oil and give them a gentle toss, ensuring they're lightly coated.
3. Preheat your air fryer to 375°F (190°C).
4. Arrange slices in a single layer in the fryer, no overlaps here!
5. Air fry for about 8-10 minutes until they turn golden and crispy.
6. Once done, sprinkle with sea salt (and optional spices if you're feeling spicy).

NUTRITION

- **CARBS: 28g**
- **PROTEIN: 1g**
- **FAT: 2.5g**
- **FIBER: 2g**
- **OMEGA 3: 0.01g**
- **VITAMIN D: 0mcg**
- **CALCIUM: 5mg**
- **IRON: 0.6mg**

ALLERGENS & TIPS

Allergens: For those with sensitivities, these plantain chips are made in an environment where other foods might be processed. Ensure your air fryer is thoroughly cleaned if concerned about cross-contamination.

Tips: The greener the plantain, the crispier your chip. If you fancy a sweeter flavor, go for a yellow plantain, but keep an eye out as they cook faster.

HERBED EGGPLANT SLICES

85 KCAL

2 SERVINGS

15 MIN

INGREDIENTS

- One eggplant (8oz / 225g) – gotta get those veggies in!
- Olive oil spray – the healthy choice, you know?
- Fresh rosemary, finely chopped: 1 tsp (5ml)
- Fresh thyme, finely chopped: 1 tsp (5ml)
- A smidge of garlic powder
- Some good old sea salt: a sprinkle or so

NUTRITION

- **CARBS: 15g**
- **PROTEIN: 2g**
- **FAT: 2g**
- **FIBER: 6g**
- **OMEGA 3: 0.1g**
- **VITAMIN D: 0mcg**
- **CALCIUM: 15mg**
- **IRON: 0.3mg**

DIRECTIONS

1. Chop the top and tail off the eggplant. Slice that bad boy into rounds, about 1/4 inch (0.6cm) thick.
2. Let's give those slices a quick spray with olive oil.
3. Mix the rosemary, thyme, garlic powder, and sea salt together. Sprinkle this magic mix onto both sides of the slices.
4. Heat up that air fryer to 375°F (190°C).
5. Pop the slices in, ensuring they're snug but not piled on top of each other.
6. Fry 'em up for about 7 minutes each side, or until they're golden and your kitchen smells like heaven

ALLERGENS & TIPS

Allergens: Heads up for those with food sensitivities: these eggplant slices might have been exposed to common allergens if your air fryer was used for other goodies. Always make sure to clean well.

Tips: For an extra crispy finish, pat dry the eggplant slices before seasoning. And if you're looking for a bit of a zing, a splash of lemon juice post-frying won't go amiss!

PESTO-STUFFED CHERRY TOMATOES

70 KCAL

2 SERVINGS

10 MIN

INGREDIENTS

- 10 cherry tomatoes (about 5oz / 140g)
- 3 tablespoons (45ml) of low-fat pesto
- 1/4 cup (60ml) of low-fat ricotta cheese
- Olive oil spray
- A pinch of black pepper

DIRECTIONS

1. Halve the cherry tomatoes and carefully scoop out the insides.
2. In a bowl, mix the low-fat pesto with ricotta. Season with a bit of black pepper.
3. Carefully stuff each tomato half with the pesto mixture.
4. Lay out your tiny tomato delights on the air fryer tray.
5. Give them a quick spritz with olive oil spray.
6. Fire up the air fryer at 370°F (190°C) and cook for about 4-5 minutes. Just enough to get everything warm and slightly crispy.

NUTRITION

- **CARBS: 4g**
- **PROTEIN: 3g**
- **FAT: 4g**
- **FIBER: 1g**
- **OMEGA 3: 0.3g**
- **VITAMIN D: 0mcg**
- **CALCIUM: 60mg**
- **IRON: 0.4mg**

ALLERGENS & TIPS

Allergens: This dish contains dairy (ricotta) which could be problematic for those with dairy allergies or lactose intolerance; also, be mindful of nuts in certain pesto brands.

Tips: Steady hands make for neat tomato stuffing; using a small spoon or a piping bag can be a real game-changer. And for an extra twist, sprinkle a touch of grated parmesan before air frying.

SPICY ROASTED CORN ON THE COB

100 KCAL

2 SERVINGS

10 MIN

INGREDIENTS

- 2 fresh corn cobs (about 16oz total / 450g)
- Olive oil spray
- 1/2 teaspoon (2.5ml) smoked paprika
- 1/4 teaspoon (1.25ml) chili powder
- 1/4 teaspoon (1.25ml) garlic powder
- A pinch of black pepper and salt

NUTRITION

- **Carbs: 35g**
- **Protein: 28g**
- **Fat: 6g**
- **Fiber: 5g**
- **Omega 3: 0.1g**
- **Vitamin D: 0.5µg**
- **Calcium: 50mg**
- **Iron: 3mg**

DIRECTIONS

1. Rinse and pat dry the corn cobs. Brush away any stray silk.
2. Spray each corn cob lightly with olive oil.
3. Mix smoked paprika, chili powder, garlic powder, salt, and pepper in a small bowl.
4. Rub the spice mix over each corn cob, ensuring an even coat.
5. Place the cobs in the air fryer basket.
6. Cook at 400°F (205°C) for about 10 minutes, turning halfway through, until charred and tender.

ALLERGENS & TIPS

Allergens: This spicy corn recipe is quite allergy-friendly; however, always ensure your spices and olive oil spray don't contain any allergens or additives if you're particularly sensitive.

Tips: To make your corn even tastier, try squeezing a fresh lime wedge over the finished product. And hey, if you're into creamy flavors, a dab of low-fat yogurt can make a cool contrast to the spice!

CINNAMON APPLE SLICES

95 KCAL

2 SERVINGS

5 MIN

INGREDIENTS

- 2 medium-sized apples (8oz each / 225g)
- 1 teaspoon (5ml) ground cinnamon
- Olive oil spray

NUTRITION

- **CARBS: 25g**
- **PROTEIN: 0.5g**
- **FAT: 0.4g**
- **FIBER: 4g**
- **OMEGA 3: 0.01g**
- **VITAMIN D: 0mcg**
- **CALCIUM: 10mg**
- **IRON: 0.2mg**

DIRECTIONS

1. Wash and core the apples. Slice them into 1/4-inch thick rounds.
2. Spritz apple slices lightly with olive oil spray.
3. Evenly sprinkle cinnamon over the apple slices.
4. Arrange slices in a single layer in the air fryer basket.
5. Set the air fryer to 350°F (175°C) and cook for 8 minutes, or until edges curl slightly and they turn golden.

ALLERGENS & TIPS

Allergens: The primary ingredients are apples, cinnamon, and olive oil spray. Ensure the olive oil spray doesn't contain additives that might be potential allergens.

Tips: For a fun twist, try adding a pinch of nutmeg or serving with a dollop of low-fat Greek yogurt. Remember, always choose crisp apple varieties for best results!

GARLIC-LEMON ASPARAGUS SPEARS

60 KCAL

2 SERVINGS

20 MIN

INGREDIENTS

- 10 asparagus spears (medium thickness), washed and trimmed
- 1 tbsp olive oil (0.5 oz / 15 ml)
- 2 garlic cloves, finely minced
- Zest of half a lemon
- A pinch of salt and pepper

NUTRITION

- **Carbs: 4g**
- **Protein: 2g**
- **Fat: 3.5g**
- **Fiber: 2g**
- **Omega 3: 0.2g**
- **Vitamin D: 0 IU (**
- **Calcium: 27mg**
- **Iron: 2.4mg**

DIRECTIONS

1. In a bowl, mix the olive oil, minced garlic, lemon zest, salt, and pepper.
2. Toss the asparagus in this flavorful mix, ensuring they're well coated.
3. Preheat your air fryer to 375°F (190°C). Once heated, arrange the asparagus spears inside.
4. Cook for about 8 minutes or until they're tender and slightly crispy. Give 'em a shake halfway through.
5. Serve immediately. These babies are best enjoyed hot!

ALLERGENS & TIPS

Allergens: This recipe contains garlic, which some individuals may be allergic or sensitive to. Always ensure you're using fresh ingredients and be mindful of potential cross-contamination in shared kitchen spaces.

Tips: For an extra burst of flavor, you can sprinkle some grated parmesan on the asparagus in the last 2 minutes of air frying. Also, thinner asparagus might need a reduced cooking time, so keep an eye on them to prevent overcooking.

CAPRESE STUFFED PORTOBELLO MUSHROOMS

110 KCAL

2 SERVINGS

15 MIN

INGREDIENTS

- 2 large portobello mushrooms, cleaned and stems removed
- 4 cherry tomatoes, halved (8 halves / 16 halves metric)
- 1 oz (30 g) fresh mozzarella, diced
- 6 fresh basil leaves, torn
- 1/2 tsp (2.5 ml) olive oil
- Salt and pepper, to taste
- Drizzle of balsamic reduction (optional)

NUTRITION

- **Carbs: 7g**
- **Protein: 5g**
- **Fat: 6g**
- **Fiber: 1g**
- **Omega 3: 0.1g**
- **Vitamin D: 0.2mcg**
- **Calcium: 84mg**
- **Iron: 0.5mg**

DIRECTIONS

1. Clean the mushrooms and remove the gills using a spoon to create more space for the filling.
2. In a bowl, combine cherry tomatoes, diced mozzarella, basil, olive oil, salt, and pepper.
3. Stuff each mushroom with the Caprese mix.
4. Preheat the air fryer to 375°F (190°C).
5. Carefully place the stuffed mushrooms into the fryer and cook for 8-10 minutes, or until mushrooms are tender and cheese is melted.
6. Finish off with a drizzle of balsamic reduction if desired.

ALLERGENS & TIPS

Allergens: Be aware of the presence of dairy (mozzarella) in this dish. It's always a good idea to double-check all ingredients for any other potential allergens, especially if using pre-packaged items.

Tips: Enhance the flavors by allowing the Caprese mix to marinate for a bit before stuffing. And if you fancy a crispier top, sprinkle a touch of grated parmesan during the last two minutes of frying!

SESAME-GINGER EDAMAME PODS

150 KCAL

2 SERVINGS

10 MIN

INGREDIENTS

- 1 cup (about 150g) edamame pods, fresh or frozen
- 1 tsp (5ml) sesame oil
- 1 tsp (5ml) fresh ginger, finely grated
- 1 tbsp (15ml) low-sodium soy sauce
- 1 tsp (5ml) sesame seeds
- A pinch of chili flakes (optional)
- Salt, to taste

NUTRITION

- **Carbs: 10g**
- **Protein: 8g**
- **Fat: 5g**
- **Fiber: 4g**
- **Omega 3: 0.3g**
- **Vitamin D: 0mcg**
- **Calcium: 50mg**
- **Iron: 1.5mg**

DIRECTIONS

1. In a mixing bowl, whisk together sesame oil, grated ginger, soy sauce, and chili flakes.
2. Toss in the edamame pods ensuring they're well coated.
3. Preheat the air fryer to 390°F (200°C).
4. Once heated, place the marinated edamame pods in the fryer basket in a single layer.
5. Air-fry for 8-10 minutes, shaking halfway, until they're golden and crispy.
6. Transfer to a serving bowl, sprinkle with sesame seeds, and a pinch of salt.

ALLERGENS & TIPS

Allergens: This recipe contains soy from edamame and soy sauce. It's always crucial to ensure none of the ingredients have been cross-contaminated with allergens during processing.

Tips: For a spicier kick, sprinkle in some more chili flakes, or try adding a drizzle of chili oil after frying. Fresh ginger makes all the difference, so don't skimp on it!

CRISPY COCONUT-CAULIFLOWER

120 KCAL

2 SERVINGS

15 MIN

INGREDIENTS

- 1 cup (about 150g) cauliflower florets
- 2 tbsp (30ml) coconut milk
- 1/3 cup (30g) unsweetened shredded coconut
- 1/4 tsp (1.25ml) turmeric powder
- Salt, to taste

NUTRITION

- **Carbs: 8g**
- **Protein: 2g**
- **Fat: 7g**
- **Fiber: 4g**
- **Omega 3: 0.1g**
- **Vitamin D: 0mcg**
- **Calcium: 20mg**
- **Iron: 0.8mg**

DIRECTIONS

1. Rinse cauliflower florets and pat dry.
2. Dip each floret into coconut milk ensuring it's lightly coated.
3. Roll the florets in shredded coconut until evenly covered.
4. Sprinkle with turmeric and salt.
5. Preheat the air fryer to 375°F (190°C).
6. Place the coated cauliflower florets in the fryer basket in one layer.
7. Air-fry for 10 minutes or until they turn a golden hue.

ALLERGENS & TIPS

Allergens: This dish contains coconut. Always ensure to double-check for any cross-contaminants, especially if using store-bought coconut milk or shreds.

Tips: Using fresh cauliflower ensures a crisper outcome. For an added kick, you might want to mix in a pinch of paprika with turmeric!

HONEY-MUSTARD BRUSSELS SPROUT CHIPS

110 KCAL

2 SERVINGS

10 MIN

INGREDIENTS

- 8 oz (about 227g) Brussels sprouts
- 1 tbsp (15ml) honey
- 1 tbsp (15ml) Dijon mustard
- A pinch of salt
- A pinch of black pepper

NUTRITION

- **Carbs: 14g**
- **Protein: 3g**
- **Fat: 1g**
- **Fiber: 4g**
- **Omega 3: 0.2g**
- **Vitamin D: 0mcg**
- **Calcium: 28mg**
- **Iron: 1.2mg**

DIRECTIONS

1. Hey, start off by washing those Brussels sprouts. Done? Cool, now trim the stem and peel the leaves.
2. In a nice little bowl, mix that sweet honey with the Dijon mustard. Whisk it well!
3. Toss the sprout leaves into the honey-mustard mix. Make sure they're all covered.
4. Season with salt and pepper, giving them that perfect taste.
5. Fire up the air fryer! Set it to 375°F (190°C).
6. Get those leaves in, spread 'em out.
7. Let them fry for about 5-7 minutes. Keep an eye, and you'll see them turning golden and crispy!

ALLERGENS & TIPS

Allergens: Watch out! This dish contains mustard. You know, some folks might be allergic. Always good to be sure, especially if you've got guests.

Tips: The trick is in the peeling. Make sure you get as many leaves as possible from each sprout. More leaves, more chips! And remember, fresh Brussels sprouts make the crispiest chips!

TANGY PICKLE FRIES

90 KCAL

2 SERVINGS

5 MIN

INGREDIENTS

- 4 large pickles (16 oz/453g)
- 1 tbsp olive oil (15ml)
- 1/4 tsp smoked paprika (1g)
- A pinch of garlic powder
- A smidgen of sea salt

DIRECTIONS

1. Slice pickles into thin fry-like strips.
2. In a bowl, mix the olive oil, paprika, garlic powder, and salt.
3. Gently toss the pickle slices in this mixture until they're all jazzed up.
4. Heat the air fryer to 400°F (205°C).
5. Arrange your pickled pals in a single layer, ensuring they aren't too crowded.
6. Fry for about 8-10 minutes, or until they're golden and slightly crispy.

NUTRITION

- **Carbs: 6g**
- **Protein: 1g**
- **Fat: 4g**
- **Fiber: 1g**
- **Omega 3: 0.1g**
- **Vitamin D: 0mcg**
- **Calcium: 25mg**
- **Iron: 0.5mg**

ALLERGENS & TIPS

Allergens: For those with food sensitivities, remember these pickle fries contain pickled ingredients which sometimes include mustard seeds or other allergens depending on the pickle brand.

Tips: For the crispiest outcome, ensure your pickle strips are patted dry before tossing in the mixture. And hey, a side of low-fat yogurt dip complements these tangy treats perfectly!

GARLIC-PARMESAN ARTICHOKE HEARTS

110 KCAL

2 SERVINGS

10 MIN

INGREDIENTS

- 1 can of artichoke hearts (14 oz/397g), drained
- 1 tbsp olive oil (15ml)
- 1 garlic clove, minced
- 1 tbsp parmesan cheese, grated (15g)
- Pinch of black pepper
- A whisper of dried basil

DIRECTIONS

1. Let's kick things off by patting those artichoke hearts dry with a paper towel.
2. Next, in a jazzy little mixing bowl, combine the olive oil and minced garlic.
3. Now, give those artichoke hearts a good toss in that garlic mix – make sure they get a good coat.
4. Pop on your air fryer and preheat it to 380°F (190°C).
5. Carefully place the artichoke hearts in, making sure they're not snuggling too close.
6. Air fry for about 5-7 minutes or until they look golden and smell heavenly.
7. Once out, while they're still hot, sprinkle them with parmesan, pepper, and basil.

NUTRITION

- **Carbs: 8g**
- **Protein: 3g**
- **Fat: 7g**
- **Fiber: 5g**
- **Omega 3: 0.2g**
- **Vitamin D: 0mcg**
- **Calcium: 60mg**
- **Iron: 1.2mg**

ALLERGENS & TIPS

Allergens: Heads up, folks! This dish contains dairy from parmesan cheese, so be wary if you or your loved ones are lactose intolerant or allergic to dairy.

Tips: To enhance the flavors, let's add a dash of lemon zest or a squeeze of lemon juice after frying. And if you're a fan of crispy, let the artichokes sit a minute longer in the fryer, but keep an eye on them!

105 KCAL

2 SERVINGS

10 MIN

SPICED CARROT STICKS WITH YOGURT DIP

INGREDIENTS

- 4 large carrots (peeled and sliced into sticks)
- 1/2 tsp smoked paprika (2.5ml)
- 1/2 tsp ground cumin (2.5ml)
- 1 tbsp olive oil (15ml)
- 1/2 cup plain Greek yogurt (120ml)
- 1 small garlic clove, minced
- 1 tbsp fresh dill, chopped (15g)
- Salt and pepper, to taste

NUTRITION

- **Carbs: 12g**
- **Protein: 4g**
- **Fat: 4g**
- **Fiber: 3g**
- **Omega 3: 0.1g**
- **Vitamin D: 0mcg**
- **Calcium: 90mg**
- **Iron: 0.6mg**

DIRECTIONS

1. Preheat your trusty air fryer to 380°F (190°C).
2. Toss carrot sticks with paprika, cumin, olive oil, and a pinch of salt and pepper.
3. Lay carrot sticks in the air fryer, making sure not to overcrowd.
4. Fry those beauties for about 10 minutes, giving them a little shake midway.
5. Meanwhile, in a bowl, stir together Greek yogurt, minced garlic, dill, and season with salt and pepper.
6. Once carrots are done, serve 'em up with that tasty yogurt dip.

ALLERGENS & TIPS

Allergens: Keep an eye out, folks! This dish has dairy (from the Greek yogurt) and may affect those sensitive to lactose or with dairy allergies.

Tips: For an extra zing, squeeze a hint of lemon juice into the yogurt dip, and if you're seeking more crispiness for your carrots, just add an extra minute or two to the fry time. Easy peasy!

TERIYAKI TOFU NUGGETS

130 KCAL

2 SERVINGS

15 MIN

INGREDIENTS

- 7 oz firm tofu (200g), drained and cut into bite-sized cubes
- 2 tbsp teriyaki sauce (30ml)
- 1/4 cup breadcrumbs (60ml)
- 1 tsp sesame seeds (5ml)
- 1/4 tsp black pepper (1.25ml)
- Olive oil spray, for a light coat

NUTRITION

- **Carbs: 15g**
- **Protein: 8g**
- **Fat: 4g**
- **Fiber: 1g**
- **Omega 3: 0.3g**
- **Vitamin D: 0mcg**
- **Calcium: 130mg**
- **Iron: 1.5mg**

DIRECTIONS

1. Let's kick things off by marinating tofu cubes in teriyaki sauce for about 10 minutes. The longer, the tangier!
2. While Mr. Tofu is soaking up the goodness, mix breadcrumbs, sesame seeds, and black pepper in a separate bowl.
3. Roll those tofu cubes in the breadcrumb mixture until they're looking snazzy.
4. Place your nuggets in the air fryer basket. Give 'em a light spray with olive oil.
5. Air fry at 370°F (188°C) for 12 minutes. Don't forget to shake the basket halfway!

ALLERGENS & TIPS

Allergens: Hey there, food lover! This dish contains soy (from tofu) and gluten (from breadcrumbs), so if you've got allergies, be sure to tread carefully.

Tips: For an extra crispy touch, you can use panko breadcrumbs instead. If you're all about that spicy life, toss in a pinch of chili flakes to the breadcrumb mix. Hot, hot, hot!

66

AIR FRYER S'MORES PASTRIES

160 KCAL

2 SERVINGS

10 MIN

INGREDIENTS

- 2 whole wheat pastry sheets (5x5 inches; 13x13 cm)
- 1/4 cup mini marshmallows (60ml)
- 1/4 cup dark chocolate chips (60ml)
- 1/4 cup crushed graham crackers (60ml)
- Cooking spray

NUTRITION

- **Carbs: 25g**
- **Protein: 3g**
- **Fat: 6g**
- **Fiber: 2g**
- **Omega 3: 0.1g**
- **Vitamin D: 0.2mcg**
- **Calcium: 20mg**
- **Iron: 1.2mg**

DIRECTIONS

1. Lay out your pastry sheets on a flat surface.
2. In the center, sprinkle half the chocolate chips, marshmallows, and graham crackers on each pastry.
3. Fold the pastries to form a triangle. Press the edges with a fork.
4. Lightly spray both sides with cooking spray.
5. Pop them into the air fryer at 350°F (175°C) for about 6 minutes or until golden brown.

ALLERGENS & TIPS

Allergens: Heads up, pastry pals! This delightful treat contains wheat (from pastry and graham crackers), dairy (from chocolate), and might have traces of nuts depending on your chocolate brand.

Tips: For an even healthier twist, opt for low-fat dark chocolate chips. And here's a sneaky tip: lightly dust with cinnamon for a warm, spicy kick.

VANILLA BEAN POUND CAKE

180 KCAL

2 SERVINGS

15 MIN

INGREDIENTS

- 1/3 cup + 1 tbsp whole wheat flour (90ml + 15ml)
- 2 tbsp coconut sugar (30ml)
- 1/2 vanilla bean, scraped or 1/2 tsp vanilla bean paste (2.5ml)
- 1 large egg
- 2 tbsp unsweetened applesauce (30ml)
- 1/4 tsp baking powder (1.25ml)
- Pinch of salt
- 1 tbsp almond milk (15ml)
- Cooking spray

NUTRITION

- **Carbs: 26g**
- **Protein: 5g**
- **Fat: 3g**
- **Fiber: 2g**
- **Omega 3: 0.1g**
- **Vitamin D: 0.5mcg**
- **Calcium: 45mg**
- **Iron: 1.4mg**

DIRECTIONS

1. In a mixing bowl, combine the flour, coconut sugar, salt, and baking powder.
2. Toss in the vanilla bean paste or scraped vanilla bean.
3. Mix in the egg and applesauce until smooth.
4. Slowly add the almond milk, ensuring the batter remains thick but pourable.
5. Pour the mixture into a small, air fryer-safe cake tin sprayed with cooking spray.
6. Air fry at 320°F (160°C) for 12 minutes, or until a toothpick comes out clean.

ALLERGENS & TIPS

Allergens: This vanilla pound cake contains wheat and egg. And hey, if you're allergic to nuts, watch out for almond milk brands that might have cross-contamination.

Tips: Wanna get fancy? Add some berries on top for a fruity twist, or drizzle with a bit of honey for a natural sweet kick.

CRUNCHY OREO COOKIES

110 KCAL

2 SERVINGS

10 MIN

INGREDIENTS

- 4 Oreo cookies
- 1/4 cup Greek yogurt (60ml)
- 2 tbsp whole wheat breadcrumbs (30ml)
- A dash of cinnamon
- Cooking spray

DIRECTIONS

1. Preheat the air fryer to 375°F (190°C).
2. Dip each Oreo into the Greek yogurt, ensuring it's fully covered.
3. Mix the breadcrumbs with cinnamon.
4. Coat each yogurt-dipped Oreo in the breadcrumb mixture.
5. Spray the cookies lightly with cooking spray.
6. Place in the air fryer and cook for 5 minutes or until they're golden and crispy.

NUTRITION

- **Carbs: 18g**
- **Protein: 3g**
- **Fat: 3g**
- **Fiber: 1g**
- **Omega 3: 0.05g**
- **Vitamin D: 0.2mcg**
- **Calcium: 30mg**
- **Iron: 1mg**

ALLERGENS & TIPS

Allergens: This recipe includes wheat (from Oreos and breadcrumbs), milk (from Greek yogurt), and soy. Some Oreo variants may also contain nuts, so be sure to check the packaging.

Tips: For a little twist, mix in a bit of cocoa powder or vanilla essence with your breadcrumbs. It adds an extra layer of flavor that complements the Oreo beautifully.

BLUEBERRY HAND PIES

180 KCAL

2 SERVINGS

15 MIN

INGREDIENTS

- 1/2 cup fresh blueberries (120ml)
- 1 tsp honey (5ml)
- 1/4 tsp lemon zest
- 2 small whole wheat tortillas (6-inch/15cm diameter)
- 1 tsp cornstarch (5ml)
- Cooking spray

NUTRITION

- **Carbs: 35g**
- **Protein: 4g**
- **Fat: 3g**
- **Fiber: 4g**
- **Omega 3: 0.03g**
- **Vitamin D: 0mcg**
- **Calcium: 40mg**
- **Iron: 1mg**

DIRECTIONS

1. In a bowl, mix the blueberries, honey, and lemon zest. Set aside.
2. Dissolve cornstarch in a tiny bit of water and stir it into the blueberry mixture. This'll make your filling thick and lush.
3. Lay out the tortillas and place half of the blueberry mixture on one half of each tortilla.
4. Fold tortillas to seal in those sweet blue gems, press the edges lightly.
5. Give 'em a quick spray with cooking spray.
6. Slide them into the air fryer and cook at 350°F (175°C) for about 7 minutes or until crispy and golden brown.

ALLERGENS & TIPS

Allergens: This treat contains wheat from the tortillas and may have traces of other allergens depending on the brand. Always best to check the labels if you're uncertain.

Tips: Sprinkling a bit of cinnamon or nutmeg onto your blueberry mix can jazz things up. Or, for a little crunch, add some chopped nuts.

GLAZED CINNAMON ROLLS

220 KCAL

2 SERVINGS

20 MIN

INGREDIENTS

- 1 cup whole wheat flour (240ml)
- 1/2 tsp active dry yeast (2.5ml)
- 1/4 cup warm water (60ml)
- 1 tsp cinnamon (5ml)
- 1 tbsp brown sugar (15ml)
- Cooking spray

For Glaze:

- 1 tbsp Greek yogurt (15ml)
- 1 tsp honey (5ml)

NUTRITION

- **Carbs: 45g**
- **Protein: 6g**
- **Fat: 3g**
- **Fiber: 4g**
- **Omega 3: 0.02g**
- **Vitamin D: 0.1mcg**
- **Calcium: 45mg**
- **Iron: 2mg**

DIRECTIONS

1. Mix flour and yeast. Slowly add warm water until a soft dough forms.
2. Roll out dough on a floured surface to about 1/4 inch (0.6 cm) thick.
3. Sprinkle cinnamon and brown sugar evenly over the surface.
4. Gently roll the dough into a log and slice into 2 equal parts.
5. Spray each roll with cooking spray.
6. Air fry at 350°F (175°C) for 10 minutes, or until they turn golden.
7. For glaze, mix Greek yogurt and honey. Drizzle over warm rolls.

ALLERGENS & TIPS

Allergens: This delightful dessert contains wheat due to the flour. The Greek yogurt may also be a dairy allergen, so always double-check labels for any hidden components.

Tips: Add a dash of vanilla extract to the glaze for a richer flavor. Letting the rolls cool a bit before glazing helps it set nicely.

COCONUT SHRIMP DESSERT TACOS

220 KCAL

2 SERVINGS

15 MIN

INGREDIENTS

- 6 large shrimps, peeled and deveined (around 6oz/170g)
- 1/4 cup unsweetened shredded coconut (60ml)
- 1/4 cup whole wheat flour (60ml)
- 1/4 cup low-fat coconut milk (60ml)
- 2 small whole wheat tortillas
- 1/2 tsp vanilla extract (2.5ml)
- A pinch of sea salt
- 1 tbsp honey (15ml)
- Cooking spray

NUTRITION

- **Carbs: 28g**
- **Protein: 12g**
- **Fat: 6g**
- **Fiber: 3g**
- **Omega 3: 0.1g**
- **Vitamin D: 0.5mcg**
- **Calcium: 50mg**
- **Iron: 1mg**

DIRECTIONS

1. Dip each shrimp into the coconut milk mixed with vanilla, then coat with flour, and finally with shredded coconut.
2. Lay shrimp flat in the air fryer basket, leaving space between each.
3. Air fry at 375°F (190°C) for 8 minutes or until golden.
4. Warm the tortillas briefly in the fryer, just about 1 minute.
5. Place 3 shrimp on each tortilla, drizzle with honey and a sprinkle of sea salt.

ALLERGENS & TIPS

Allergens: For our friends with dietary concerns, this treat has shrimp (seafood), wheat from tortillas, and coconut. Always double-check labels and be aware of cross-contaminations.

Tips: If you're craving a zest, a little squeeze of lime works wonders on these dessert tacos! Adjust honey based on sweetness preference.

72

PINEAPPLE FRITTERS

150 KCAL

2 SERVINGS

20 MIN

INGREDIENTS

- 4 pineapple rings (around 4oz/115g total)
- 1/4 cup whole wheat flour (60ml)
- 1/4 cup sparkling water (60ml)
- 1/2 tsp cinnamon (2.5ml)
- 1 tbsp honey (15ml) for drizzling
- Cooking spray

NUTRITION

- **Carbs: 36g**
- **Protein: 2g**
- **Fat: 0.5g**
- **Fiber: 2g**
- **Omega 3: 0g**
- **Vitamin D: 0mcg**
- **Calcium: 20mg**
- **Iron: 0.8mg**

DIRECTIONS

1. Mix the whole wheat flour, sparkling water, and cinnamon to make a batter.
2. Dunk each pineapple ring into the batter, ensuring a thin coat.
3. Place the coated pineapple rings in the air fryer basket with space between.
4. Spray a smidge of cooking spray over the rings.
5. Air fry at 375°F (190°C) for 8-10 minutes or until golden brown.
6. Serve warm, and oh! Don't forget that honey drizzle.

ALLERGENS & TIPS

Allergens: Watch out, these fritters contain wheat from the flour. Just a heads-up to double-check the ingredient list if you're being mindful of allergies.

Tips: These fritters are best fresh but can be reheated if needed. Maybe pair with some low-fat vanilla yogurt for a smooth contrast!

PUMPKIN SPICE DONUTS

180 KCAL

2 SERVINGS

15 MIN

INGREDIENTS

- 1/2 cup whole wheat flour (120ml)
- 1/4 cup pumpkin puree (60ml)
- 2 tbsp maple syrup (30ml)
- 1/2 tsp baking powder (2.5ml)
- 1/4 tsp pumpkin spice (1.25ml)
- Pinch of salt
- Cooking spray

DIRECTIONS

1. In a bowl, mix together flour, pumpkin puree, maple syrup, baking powder, pumpkin spice, and that pinch of salt.
2. Get that dough shaped into two beautiful donuts.
3. Pop those donuts into the air fryer basket, giving them some room to breathe.
4. Mist them with a hint of cooking spray.
5. Let 'em fry at 350°F (175°C) for about 8 minutes, or till they're looking all golden and tempting.
6. Once done, let cool a tad and then, well, devour!

NUTRITION

- **Carbs: 42g**
- **Protein: 5g**
- **Fat: 1g**
- **Fiber: 4g**
- **Omega 3: 0.2g**
- **Vitamin D: 0mcg**
- **Calcium: 55mg**
- **Iron: 1.5mg**

ALLERGENS & TIPS

Allergens: For folks watching out for allergies, these donuts do contain wheat from the flour, and you might wanna ensure other ingredients are free from cross-contamination.

Tips: Fancy a glaze? Mix some Greek yogurt with a tad more maple syrup. It'll elevate the donut game and keep things on the healthier side!

Printed in Great Britain
by Amazon